FOR JILL

Except where otherwise designated, the text is from the Today's English Version of the New Testament and Psalm. Copyright © American Bible Society 1966, 1970, 1971.

Copyright © MCMLXXII
The C. R. Gibson Company, Norwalk, Connecticut
All rights reserved
Printed in the United States of America
Library of Congress Catalog Number: 72-78466
ISBN 0-8378-2003-0

Dimensions of God's Love

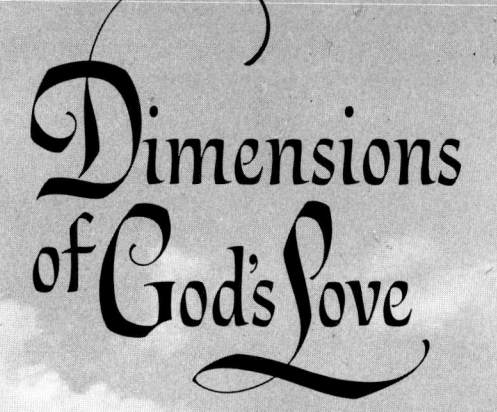

as set forth
in selected portions
of HOLY SCRIPTURE

COMPILED AND ILLUSTRATED
BY ROYAL V. CARLEY

The C. R. Gibson Company, *Publishers*
Norwalk, Connecticut

I may be able to speak the languages of men and even of angels, but if I have not love, my speech is no more than a noisy gong or a clanging bell.

1 Cor. 13:1

I may have the gift of inspired preaching;
I may have all knowledge and understand all
secrets; I may have all the faith needed to
move mountains —
but if I have not love, I am nothing.

1 Cor. 13:2

I may give away everything I have, and even give up my body to be burned — but if I have not love, it does me no good.

1 Cor. 13:3

Love is patient and kind; love is not jealous, or conceited, or proud; love is not ill-mannered, or selfish, or irritable; love does not keep a record of wrongs; love is not happy with evil, but is happy with the truth.

1 Cor. 13:4-6

Love is eternal. There are inspired messages, but they are temporary; there are gifts of speaking, but they will cease; there is knowledge, but it will pass. For our gifts of knowledge and of inspired messages are only partial; but when what is perfect comes, then what is partial disappears. When I was a child, my speech, feelings, and thinking were all those of a child; now that I am a man, I have no more use for childish ways. What we see now is like the dim image in a mirror; then we shall see face to face. What I know now is only partial; then it will be complete, as complete as God's knowledge of me. Meanwhile these three remain: faith, hope, and love; and the greatest of these is love.

1 Cor. 13:8-13

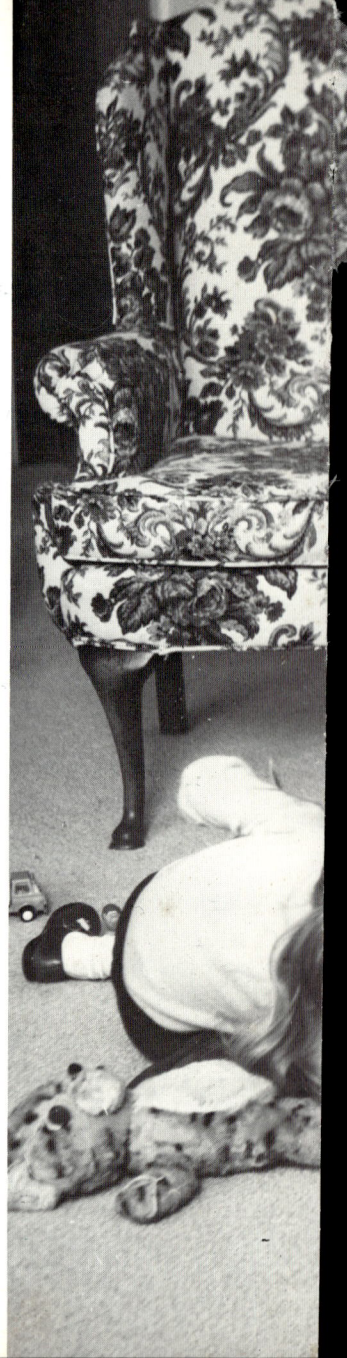

'I was hungry and you fed me, thirsty and you gave me drink; I was a stranger and you received me in your homes, naked and you clothed me; I was sick and you took care of me, in prison and you visited me.'
The righteous will then answer him: 'When, Lord, did we ever see you hungry and feed you, or thirsty and give you drink? When did we ever see you a stranger and welcome you in our homes, or naked and clothe you? When did we ever see you sick or in prison, and visit you?' The King will answer back, 'I tell you, indeed, whenever you did this for one of these poorest brothers of mine, you did it for me!'

Matt. 25:35-40

Ruth said, Intreat me not to leave thee, or to return from following after thee: for whither thou goest, I will go; and where thou lodgest, I will lodge: thy people shall be my people, and thy God my God: Where thou diest, will I die, and there will I be buried: the Lord do so to me, and more also, if ought but death part thee and me.

                                    Ruth 1:16-17 (K.J.V.)

But the Spirit produces love, joy, peace, patience, kindness, goodness, faithfulness, humility, and self-control. There is no law against such things as these.

Gal. 5:22-23

Every husband must love his wife as himself, and every wife must respect her husband.
Eph. 5:33

Children, it is your Christian duty to obey your parents, for this is the right thing to do. "Honor your father and mother" is the first commandment that has a promise added: "so that all may be well with you, and you may live a long time in the land."
Eph. 6:1-3

Thy wife shall be as a fruitful vine by the sides of thine house: Thy children like olive plants round about thy table.
Behold, that thus shall the man be blessed that feareth the Lord.
Psa. 128:3-4 (K.J.V.)

For I am certain that nothing can separate us from his love: neither death nor life; neither angels nor other heavenly rulers or powers; neither the present nor the future; neither the world above nor the world below — there is nothing in all creation that will ever be able to separate us from the love of God which is ours through Christ Jesus our Lord.
Rom. 8:38-39

My beloved spake, and said
 unto me,
  Rise up, my love, my fair one,
  and come away.
For, lo, the winter is past,
 the rain is over and gone;
The flowers appear on the earth;
 the time of the singing of birds
  is come,
And the voice of the turtle
 is heard in our land;
The fig tree putteth forth her
  green figs,
 and the vines with the tender
 grape give a good smell.
Arise, my love, my fair one,
 and come away.
          Song. Sol. 2:10-13 (K.J.V.)

Dear friends! Let us love one another, for love comes from God. Whoever loves is a child of God and knows God. Whoever does not love does not know God, because God is love. This is how God showed his love for us: he sent his only Son into the world that we might have life through him. This is what love is: it is not that we have loved God, but that he loved us and sent his Son to be the means by which our sins are forgiven. Dear friends, if this is how God loved us, then we should love one another.

1 John 4:7-11